THE BIG BAD WOLF GOES TO SCHOOL

MISS SHERRY

Copyright © 2023 by Miss Sherry

All rights reserved. No part of this book may be reproduced or used in any manner without written permission of the copyright owner except for the use of quotations in a book review.
For more information, contact:

FIRST EDITION

978-1-80541-404-9 (paperback)
978-1-80541-405-6 (ebook)

Warning! Although this story is fun to read and share, we **must never** perform parts of this story on each other or on other children in real life; this would be bullying and harmful to other children.

This story is fun and entertaining, but in real life, we have playground supervisors, teachers, lunch-time supervisors, monitors and other staff members that we trust all around school that you can report an intruder to. There are no Big, Bad Wolves in real life, but there are bad people with bad intentions and we must be careful of them.

We must remember that in real life, if you see an intruder (like a Big, Bad Wolf) or anyone who should not be there, you must tell a grown-up that you trust straight away.

This doesn't mean just in your school or playground. It could be in your homes, in the corridor of your building, in places where you play or even while out shopping. If there is anyone lurking nearby watching you or acting strangely, basically, if someone is acting like a Big Bad Wolf anywhere, be a hero by telling a trusted grown-up immediately.

With Special Thanks to
Hi3 Entertainment Network Team;

Steven Molyneaux
Gavin Roberts
Martin Monov
Joseph Allison

One day, the Big, Bad Wolf went to a school,
Lord knows what he was thinking, that silly old fool.
He climbed over the gates and slipped through the doors,
He tiptoed passed Reception, on his massive, grey paws.
Sneaking onto the playground, he found a place to hide,
He waited for playtime and for all the children to arrive.

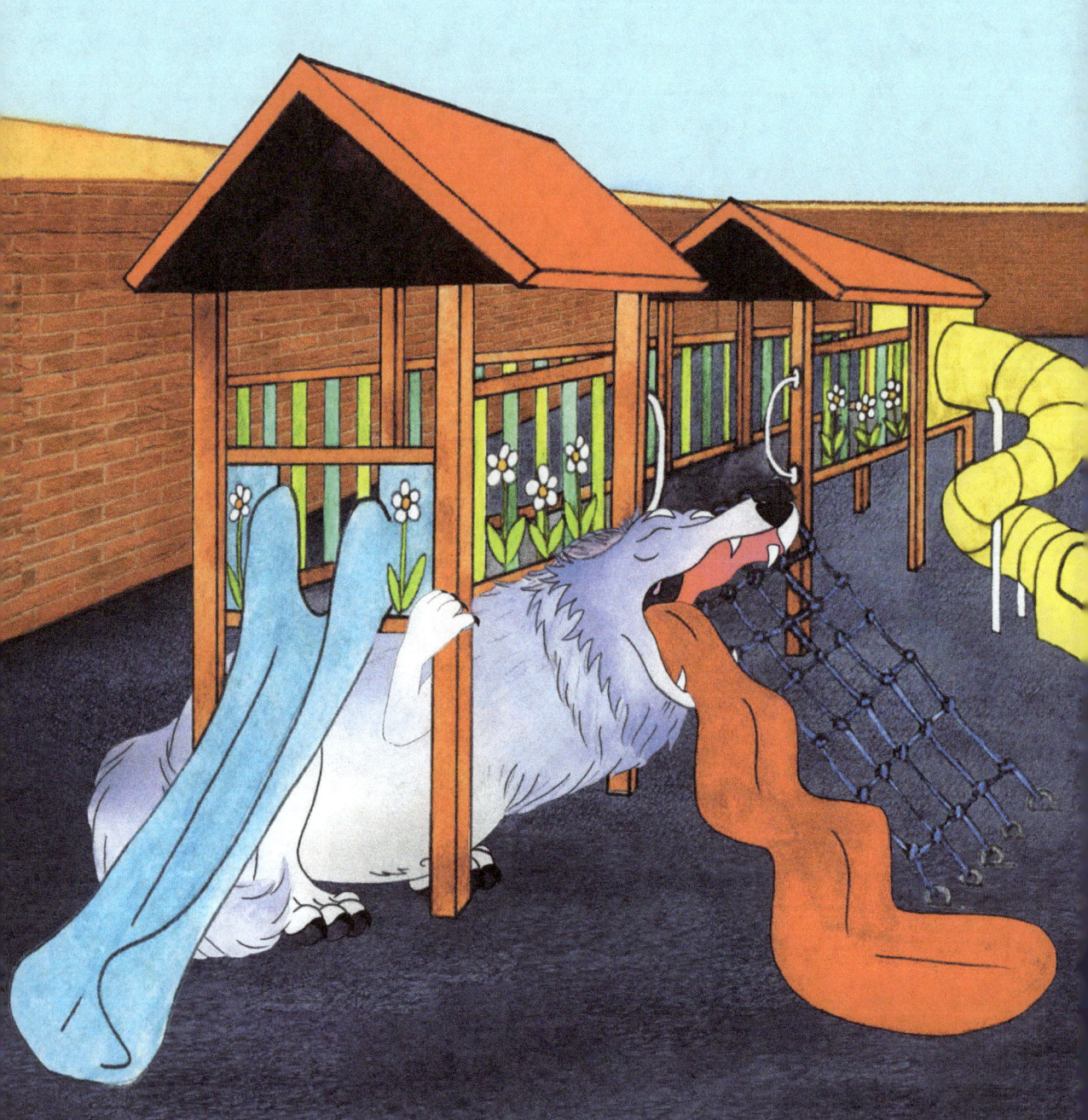

Suddenly, a bell rang, and children started to come out.

The Wolf, getting excited, licked his big, long snout.

He spotted some little girls who were starting to have a race.

The Wolf opened his mouth wide, ready, as they picked up the pace,

Hoping that the children would run directly into his embrace!
Instead, out of nowhere, a football suddenly walloped him in the face!
That silly old Wolf never managed to nab a child at all,
Only got horribly smacked in the face with a ball!

The Wolf became angry; he leapt out from hiding.
His face sore, he snarled, his eyes flashed like lightning.
Startled, the children darted, running and screaming.
The Wolf watched their terror, his eyes still gleaming.
"Mwahahah! Now I'm going to eat you all!" he laughed.
However, looking around again, he suddenly felt daft.

The children swiftly changed, re-assembling at a distance,
They had all banded together, forming a giant resistance!
"What?" yelped the Wolf, as he became confounded,
Seeing that there were hundreds of them, he was just surrounded.

"Get him!"
someone shouted; the children all ran.
"Oh no!" cried the Wolf, realising this was a stupid plan.

A stampede of children formed – the situation had become deadly.

He couldn't get out, he couldn't get away, there were just far too many.

They lassoed him with skipping ropes in a mass wolf-hunting frenzy.
Tangled up, the Wolf fell down with sucker darts all over his belly.

"Why are you here?" they asked. "Are you a fiend or a friend?
Were you really going to eat us or was it all just pretend?"
"Oh, children! Don't be silly!" he said, trying to talk meekly,
Still drooling from his grin, yet still smiling sweetly.
"You're a nasty Bad Wolf!" they yelled. "Eating children is beastly!
We'll show you, Bad Wolf, what it is to be nasty and greedy!"

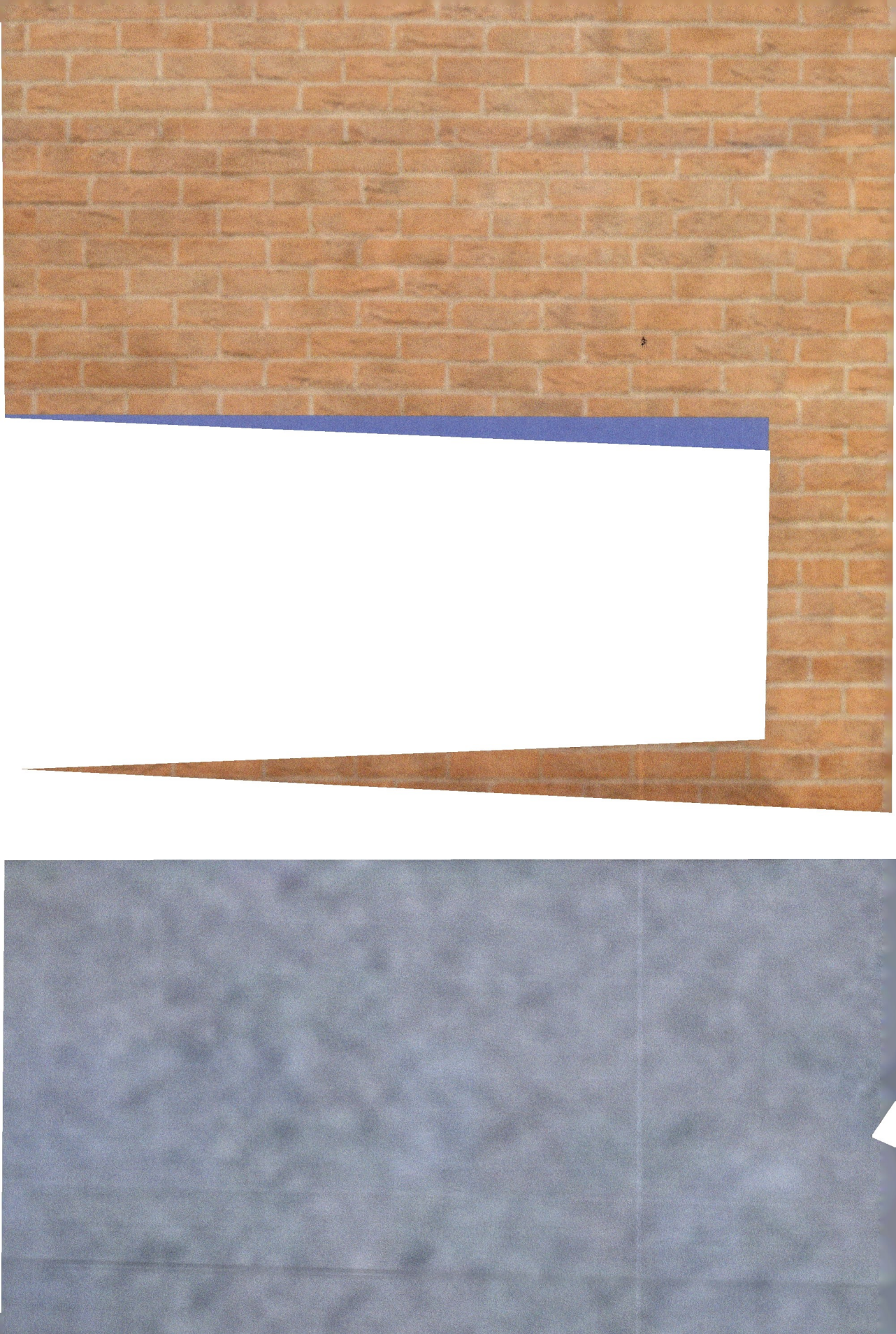

"We are like a giant family," they said, "we care about each other,
We keep each other safe and protect one another.
We're brave, we stick together, we know you're a stranger,
We know what you are ... what you eat, and the danger.

"If you want this torture to end, tell us what's true!

We are serious! We will make you eat this cat poo!"

The Wolf didn't want to eat that; that was just yuck!

He struggled but couldn't get out. They really had him stuck.

It was no use; he had to confess he was starting to feel queasy.

Exhausted in the end, he cracked, howling deeply.

The Wolf begged, "Yes, yes! Ok, it's true!

Please don't make me eat that yucky, icky, goo!

But just look at me, what do you expect me to do?

I have mighty jaws, claws and a bushy tail too.

I'm the Big, Bad Wolf; I can't just be good!

I chased the Piglets, Grandma and Little Red Riding Hood.

Even now", he drooled, "you all look and smell so delicious to me,

I still wouldn't be able to resist a taste if you do set me free.

I can't be your friend; that's a huge contradiction.

Being big and bad is my conviction, it's my mission,

It's tradition, it's even in my job description!"

"Listen up, Wolf!" they hailed. "Open up those big ears.

We don't tolerate behaviour like that around here!"

The Wolf was shocked - never in all of his nasty years
Had he been told off like this and reduced to baby Wolfy tears!
The Wolf's big smile was gone; now he only frowned,
As the children all cheered, "Let's get him off the playground!"

"Goodbye, Mr. Wolf, you are not cool,
Badness and nastiness aren't welcome here in our school."
They sent him on his way, booting him out the door.
They warned him, "Mr. Wolf, next time, it will be war!"
The Wolf quickly skulked off, running away.
The children all cheered, "Yay!" and "Hip-Hip Hooray!"

The Wolf was upset but very glad that he'd got away.

He knew he would be back at that school again someday.

He remembered the stampede hunt, the poop and the ball to his face;

He thought maybe the playground wasn't such a safe place.

He thought perhaps he needed a better plan for this crime,

Because he never quits, so he'll see you next time.

ADDITIONAL EXTRAS FOR PARENTS AND TEACHERS

STRANGER DANGER LESSON PLAN 1

Learning Objective: To discuss and plan **Stranger Danger Safety Rules**

Have a 'Circle-Time session' with your class or children - sitting in a circle, taking turns to talk, pass an object around like a small ornament or a teddy bear. The person holding the object is allowed to talk.

Warm-up: Starting alphabetically, pass the teddy bear or ornament around and each person says their name. Repeat in reverse alphabetical order. Use numbers or colours of the rainbow instead of names to change it up if you want to play again.

Before you begin:

Please allow children time to talk about things they have witnessed, even if it didn't involve them, and even if it doesn't make sense at first, as children often see or witness things but they do not always directly understand what they have seen.

Therefore, these discussions are important so that they are more aware, and also so that WE (parents, caregivers and teachers) are also more aware of any strange things that children may be witnessing. Try to avoid using names when referring to other children.

Allow children time to vent any situations that have occurred where they have ever felt 'in danger' or 'at risk' or 'pressured to do something they didn't want to do'. Allow children time to talk about things that they have witnessed, even if it is regarding another, as the information around such situations is still always important.

Circle-Time Discussion and Questions:

The Big, Bad Wolf got onto a playground - can you imagine?! We know that Big, Bad Wolves don't exist in the real world, but there are bad people out there.

- **What would a Big, Bad Wolf look like to us as a Human?**
- **How might they behave?** Discuss some ideas.
- **There are different adults around school or on a playground, so how can you tell someone is a stranger and not just a visitor?** Discuss who might visit school, what is normal and what is not normal.
- **Who is a safe grown-up to you when you are not at home?**
- **Have you ever seen someone that was acting like a Big, Bad Wolf?**
- **Have you ever felt like you were 'in danger' or 'at risk'?**
- **Have you ever 'felt pressured to do something' you didn't want to?**
- **Have you ever 'felt pressured to let someone else do something' that you didn't want them to do?**

- What did you do when that happened?
- What was the safe thing to do?
- What will you do next time something like that happens?

Remind children that they are **always allowed to say NO**, and to **never feel guilty or bad for saying no**, even if it's to an adult that they know and especially to strangers. Remind children that if they do see someone acting strangely, like a 'Big Bad Wolf', or just like some of the things discussed, they MUST find and tell a responsible grown-up immediately. They must tell a grown-up, <u>even if they do not feel as though they are in danger anymore</u>, because it could happen again. It is important because someone behaving strangely like that is still dangerous for other children too, so it must be reported. Remember, we must all work together to keep each other safe and protect ourselves.

- If a real intruder got onto your playground or into your school building, what is the protocol for <u>Stranger Danger Safety</u> at your school?
- Who do you report to if you see something on the way to school?
- Who do you report to if you see something at break-time or lunch-time?
- Who do you report to if you see something after school or on your way home?
- Who do you report to if you see something at a club or other social place, especially events outside of school?
- If the adult that you're going to report to is not available for whatever reason, what then?

If you or your children are unsure of any of these questions, then make a point of researching the answers so that the information is available when they are next at their school or club. Tell them to ask their trusted teachers or staff members to find out what the protocols are for Stranger Danger Safety at their school or club. They can even ask for a lesson or an assembly about this topic at their school.

Parents - please do not assume that your children will find out all the necessary information for you. As a parent, you have the right and responsibility to inquire about such safety precautions too.

Let the children discuss the next questions (one at a time) in pairs or as a small group <u>**before they give you an answer**</u>, as this will give you more insight into their thinking and reactions. It will give you some sense of how your children may respond to a situation, especially if you were not there at the time. Try not to intervene in the discussion; just listen; only respond and reason when they come forward with an answer.

- What about if an intruder got into your home or your building - what would the Stranger Danger Safety protocol be then?
- What about when you are playing in the park with your friends?
- What about if you were at your friend's house?
- What about other places you visit like the shops?

Make a plan of **'Stranger Danger Safety Steps'** for various places that your children regularly go to with or without you. Keep it short and simple - 2 or 3 steps at most.

Plan a couple of designated hiding places at home, for on your way to school, or other places and routes that you regularly use. Recap on all key points of the lesson.

Remind children: If you are 'in danger' and there are <u>absolutely no safe grown-ups around to help or protect you</u>, then you must hide. It is important that when you hide, the 'stranger' doesn't see where you're hiding. When it is safe, and only when it is safe, you must run and tell a grown-up that you trust immediately.

Remember, this is only for <u>specifically dangerous situations</u> when there is NO ONE at all around to help you. This is guidance to keep you safe and you must use it sensibly. Your parents must be able to trust you to do this properly and not just run off and leave your mum at the supermarket.

<u>This is for real-life dangerous situations only</u>.

In a real-life dangerous situation, you must:

- Report to a safe grown-up straight away.
- If you're <u>in danger</u> and <u>there's no one to protect you</u>, run and hide.
- Do not leave your hiding place until it is safe.

<u>Meditation activities</u>:

Heart Monitoring exercise: Ask your children to find their pulse and monitor their heart rate whilst relaxed. Do some star jumps or just jump for 30 seconds and monitor your heart rates again. Talk about the differences. Focus on breathing calmly or belly breathing for a couple of minutes and measure again for a third time.

How quickly does your heart rate speed up or settle down?

Nature Walk: Go for an outdoor nature walk together with the children. Talk about nature, the sounds you hear, how the flowers smell or how things feel in the atmosphere. Try to encourage discussions about all the senses.

ADDITIONAL EXTRAS FOR PARENTS AND TEACHERS

STRANGER DANGER LESSON PLAN 2

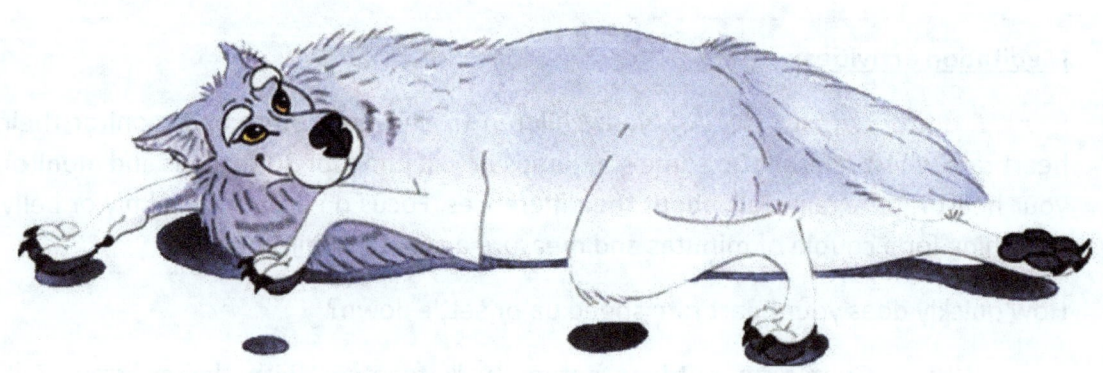

Learning Objectives:

- To recap on **Stranger Danger Safety Plans and Rules**
- To design a Stranger Danger-Proof playground.
- To create a Stranger Danger Poster.

Warm-up: Recap on some of the questions discussed in the previous Circle-time session.

- Who is a safe grown-up to you when you are away from home?
- What are the Stranger Danger Safety Rules in your school or club?
- What are the Stranger Danger Safety Rules or steps that you planned for home and/or other places?

Recap on any key points made during the previous lesson and remind children of the following:

- **To never feel guilty or be afraid of saying NO to strangers.**
- **They must report strange incidents to a trusted adult immediately.**
- **To hide when it is absolutely necessary.**

Main Activity:

Allow children the choice of either designing a Stranger Danger-Proof Playground or creating a Stranger Danger Safety Poster.

- What sensible advice could you give to another child about Stranger Danger Safety if they didn't know?
- How could the children in the story make their playground 'Stranger Danger-Proof' to keep the Big, Bad Wolf out?
- What could we do with our own playground to make it 'Stranger Danger-Proof'?

Allow the children 5-10 minutes to discuss some of their ideas together and choose which activity they would like to do. Let the children be creative and imaginative with their playground ideas. Provide children with resources and ask them to draw their ideas for a Stranger Danger-Proof playground or to create a Strange Danger Safety Poster.

Plenary:

Provide the children with some time to come up and explain their playground designs to you and/or the rest of the class. Let them talk about the functionality of their playground designs, or discuss why their poster and slogan may be interesting and informative to other children.

COMPREHENSION WORK

- Look up these words and their meaning in the dictionary:

    Confounded

    Confess

    Cracked

    Contradiction

    Conviction

- In the story, which words are used to rhyme with the word '**race**'?

    ....

- Why did the Big, Bad Wolf sneak into a school?

    ....

- How did the situation suddenly become dangerous for the Wolf?

    ....

- What did the children mean when they asked, "Are you a fiend or a friend?"

    ....

- Why did the children capture and threaten the Big, Bad Wolf?

    ....

- How did the children know that the Wolf was lying?

    ....

- How did the children warn the Wolf? What words did they use?

    ....

- Do you feel that the Big, Bad Wolf learned his lesson?

    ....

www.ingramcontent.com/pod-product-compliance
Lightning Source LLC
Chambersburg PA
CBHW081237080526
44587CB00022B/3979